A Small Handbook
of Mental Health

A Small Handbook
of Mental Health

PORTAL TO A NEW LIFE

Marcia A. Murphy

Foreword by Russell Noyes Jr.

RESOURCE *Publications* · Eugene, Oregon

A SMALL HANDBOOK OF MENTAL HEALTH
Portal to a New Life

Resource Publications
An Imprint of Wipf and Stock Publishers
199 W. 8th Ave., Suite 3
Eugene, OR 97401

www.wipfandstock.com

PAPERBACK ISBN: 978-1-6667-5332-5
HARDCOVER ISBN: 978-1-6667-5333-2
EBOOK ISBN: 978-1-6667-5334-9

AUGUST 1, 2022 4:39 PM

With gratitude to Russell Noyes Jr., MD

As the rain and the snow
come down from heaven,
and do not return to it
without watering the earth
and making it bud and flourish,
so that it yields seed for the sower and bread for the eater,
so is my word that goes out from my mouth:
It will not return to me empty,
but will accomplish what I desire
and achieve the purpose for which I sent it.

—Isa 55:10–11 NIV

Contents

Foreword

THE AUTHOR OF THIS handbook suffers from severe mental illness, schizophrenia to be specific. In the book she tells us what it is like to experience an almost life-destroying illness before going on to speak about recovery. For her this change began in the midst of a psychotic episode when God spoke to her. Although the significance of this occurrence was not immediately apparent, it eventually became the cornerstone of her recovery. So, having described the devastation of illness, she speaks about how her reliance on God gave meaning and hope for her life.

Writing by seriously mentally ill people is not common. The illness makes effective communication difficult, and for this reason, the writing they do is important. It provides insights into what the mentally ill experience. Also, it is a sharing of experience that may reduce the isolation and increase the sense of belonging among those who are ill. And fellow sufferers may pay attention and learn from the writer, in this case, how to achieve recovery.

Needless to say, serious mental illness can be devastating. It causes suffering and may result in suicide. It often prevents meaningful work or social role functioning. Social isolation is common and social stigma is an added burden. Consequences include poverty and inadequate housing. And so on.

How then is recovery to be achieved. To begin with recovery has two meanings. It usually means to regain one's health. But in the mental health field it has recently come to mean finding meaning and fulfillment despite continuing, even serious, illness. This involves taking measures to bring about change and find value and purpose. The author found recovery through her religious faith and writing. Especially important were scripture reading, prayer, and worship service attendance. Of course, what may prove effective varies from one individual to another.

The author tells her story, and in doing so gives direction and offers encouragement. And in doing this she lets the seriously mentally ill know they are not alone.

Russell Noyes Jr., MD
Professor Emeritus, Department of Psychiatry
Roy J. and Lucille A. Carver College of Medicine,
University of Iowa
July 1, 2022

Introduction

IT'S A GIFT.

One morning at the crack of dawn I realized that faith and good mental health are almost entirely gifts of grace from God. I know I've had to make some effort, too; but at times, it feels like a gift. For example, one day, out of the blue as I was standing at the bus stop, I felt uplifted, positive, and optimistic about my relationship with God, strengthening my belief in an all-powerful and all-knowing Creator. For a time, I had been thinking that God was weak or uncaring, unwilling or unable to help me with my on-going struggles with mental illness. Then things turned around that morning and I felt momentarily transformed from being submerged in an emotional, despondent hell, into a realm of joyful hope.

My prayers *do* get answered. As someone of faith who struggles with a serious mental illness, I pray for help every day. But it wasn't always like this. Early in life, most of the time, I was not very spiritual. As a child I had dreams of becoming a famous movie star in a life completely focused on myself. My parents even purchased miniature high heels and sunglasses for me to show off in. Yes! I wanted attention! I wanted to be *beautiful* and popular. All of that eventually evaporated as I grew older. The imposition of social problems was oppressive. Feeling bullied throughout my formative years, the emotional wounds cut deep into my persona.

The name-calling became internalized and self-accusatory—one reason for my negative self-image. Then I no longer wanted to be in the spotlight; I just wanted to run away and hide.

Fast forward to age eighteen and I did run away, now suffering from psychiatric illness big time, with depression, self-harm, and a desperate suicide attempt. I left home to join a quasi-religious cult (the Unification Church) and for a time was working at sites in various parts of the United States, but mostly in New York City. I emerged three and a half years later a psychotic disaster. After returning home to Iowa City, my mother helped me to obtain psychiatric care from a top-notch psychiatrist at the University of Iowa Hospitals and Clinics for treatments with medication and psychotherapy. I acquired some hope; hope to create a better future than if I had been left to struggle on my own. Without this assistance, I might have ended up homeless, starved, and, possibly, dead.

What followed was anti-psychotic and anti-depression medications, and partial rehabilitation. I moved forward but struggled with poverty, on-going social problems, and employment difficulties. Unwise relationships, unchallenging and unrewarding jobs—wrong everything. Being unable to deeply connect with God through a church community I floundered unbearably which resulted in yet another nearly successful suicide attempt at the age of thirty-nine.

This near-death event turned out to be a new beginning. During a period of physical recuperation and being started on a new medication I turned to serious reflection. Recollecting my last year in New York battling malevolent psychotic voices I then remembered the intervening, benevolent Voice in the rain saying: *Believe in Jesus Christ and you'll be saved!* This was the vision (verbal and auditory) to guide me out of the danger at that particular time and, again, later, during my entire recovery process. Things began slowly, and then by mid-life I decided to pursue writing, beginning one day by typing The Lord's Prayer on an old, electric typewriter. Typing this prayer was the way I initially refocused on God which continued for many years to follow. Writing, then, became the method I used for putting my reflections into expression, thus communicating to the world my recollections of madness, visions, and hope. And with this came healing and the beginnings of social reintegration, as well as a way to help others similarly afflicted.

I am a person with serious mental illness. Yet, through religious faith, modern medicine, and the development of good habits, I have come to understand how to maintain a healthy lifestyle and how to become a productive, self-conscious agent within the community. More importantly, my new life only began when I sought to develop a repentant, reverent relationship with God. This is the foundation of my being and subsequent basis for daily activities. Along with my writing ministry, I took on the project of being an advocate for the mentally ill in practical ways.

With this handbook I hope to increase understanding of those who suffer with mental illness, lessen stigma, and advocate for those who have few opportunities to speak out for themselves. I hope to show how despite the devastation of severe mental illness, recovery can be achieved. This handbook consists of two sections: The first is devoted to the impact of mental illness and the second is concerned with recovery. Each addresses aspects that are biological, psychological, social, and spiritual in nature. The juxtaposition of illness and recovery highlight each aspect as described through my personal narrative.

My life of adversity with schizophrenia, PTSD, and clinical depression—all serious mental illnesses—did not come without its positive benefits however. For example, because of the devastation of a psychiatric disability I then had to compensate for this loss by developing strengths of character. I learned certain lessons that would eventually bring about new behavior and thought patterns. This enabled me to overcome numerous obstacles and then continue on to achieve some limited success. The first section, *Mental Illness*, is a summary of how deeply broken a human being can be; and then in section two, *Recovery*, I revisit the factors found in section one and describe what I found helpful in achieving a rejuvenated life, one that rises up from the devastation of debilitating mental illness. Though I am willing to acknowledge that recovery is an individual matter with each person finding their own unique path; I also postulate that there are some basic universals within the human condition common to us all. I will attest to this.

I

MENTAL ILLNESS

Mental Illness
Biological

And they sat with him on the ground seven days and seven nights,
and no one spoke a word to him,
for they saw that his suffering was very great.

(JOB 2:13 ESV)

MANY PEOPLE WHO ARE afflicted with mental illness also suffer from addictions with illicit drugs and/or abuse of alcohol. I have not had this experience. The closest thing I have had with addiction was that for a while I would drink vast quantities of diet pop on a daily basis. I craved it, and it seemed to take the unconscious place of the alcohol abuse which was rampant in my immediate and extended family. I've never craved alcoholic beverages; I just tried a few drinks a few times in my youth. But I did crave diet pop and it seemed to be like an addiction.

The biological factors of food scarcity and physical health has been challenging. When I was out of the cult in my twenties and hospitalized, they said I suffered from malnutrition. So I started taking multiple vitamins and tried to eat healthy food. But my mental condition had so deteriorated, that I was not really cognizant of healthy choices. I remember eating vegetables and some fruit, but sometimes had to buy inexpensive, starchy, filler-foods because that was mostly all I could afford. However, I remember eating a lot of broccoli and opening cans of tuna fish both of which were healthy. Finding enough food to survive on, especially nutritious food, has been a near-constant struggle for most of my adult life. Finding food resources has been an on-going issue. The US government does not provide enough in Disability payments (SSDI) or Supplemental Security Income (SSI) for people to survive on. And they unjustly criminalize certain attempts to get out of the scarcity. These laws need to be changed.

Then there is the biological factor of genetics. Mental illness is a complex disorder with a multifactorial genesis; there is not just one cause and genetics plays a part. The following is what is currently known about genes in relation to schizophrenia and other mental illnesses up to, approximately, the year 2022:

> What is definitely clear is that schizophrenia and other mental illnesses do not follow simple genetic models such as a replicated identifiable abnormality in a given set of genes leading to disease. With schizophrenia it is thought that variations in many genes likely contribute to the risk of developing schizophrenia. The genetic changes can also interact with environmental factors that are associated with increased schizophrenia risk such as exposure to infections before birth, severe stress during childhood, and likely others.[1]

What about physical living quarters? Having a place to live where you do not feel threatened by other people is a major component in sound mental health. For part of my adult years, I have lived in dangerous neighborhoods where predators lurked around many corners (no delusion). People recently released from prisons could rent out units nearby and many were uncivilized and disrespectful of others. People in my apartment building have banged on walls, slammed doors violently, tore my name off of my mailbox, and stole my doormat. I have been verbally and physically threatened when I am just trying to mind my own business and keep to myself. I have also been stalked (no delusion).

1. Del D. Miller MD, email to author, 6/10/2022.

A physically decaying apartment building with cracked walls, clogged and leaking plumbing, inadequate heating or air conditioning, broken laundry machines, stoves, and ovens; all this and more, affects our daily lives. Insensitive landlords unresponsive to tenants' needs can further exacerbate our psychological problems. Many disabled people live in substandard housing overrun by pests. They may request a new air conditioner, but even though it is a hot season of the year, landlords won't supply new air conditioning units. This is abuse. And the disabled suffer. Some people arrogantly proclaim that the poor don't need air conditioning. I would suggest that they, themselves, try to go without it during dangerous summer heatwaves with temperatures above ninety degrees, reaching sometimes above one hundred, nonstop, for days at a time. I, personally, have experienced hyperthermia (bodily overheating) when my apartment was hot, which is a life-threatening condition.

So how does a person recover from mental illness in these settings? Not easily. I've resorted to keep moving on, to try a new place that would be more hospitable. Early in my life I lived in a single room rented out in a house in a decaying section of town. I had a single hot-plate for cooking. Once I experienced my bed having bugs. At the time, I shared a bathroom with two other female tenants who had their own rooms. It was cold in my room the winter and hot in the summer. By the grace of God, I eventually found better apartments and moved up in the world.

Then I was also dealing with my bodily medical issues. My psychiatric medications have had side effects such as weight gain, elevated blood sugars, and ultra-sensitivity to hot and cold room and outdoor temperatures. The blood sugar problem progressed into Type 2 diabetes. I currently control it with an oral medication. The first-generation anti-psychotic medications were not very effective, such as Stelazine, which I took for several years; it didn't help much. And as for my experience with major depression off and on, we tried several anti-depressant medications but I was unable to tolerate the side effects. Instead of using medications, I prefer to find the psychological and spiritual sources of my despair (getting to the root of the problem).

Now I am in my sixties and both of my lower extremities have severe musculoskeletal pain and weakness. Walking is very difficult and I can't be on my feet for very long. I use two crutches and own a manual wheelchair. I get easily exhausted and suffer great discomfort even when sitting or lying down. At the time of this writing, I have applied for a handicapped accessible apartment unit. As a result of these disabilities, my mobility is challenged daily and I struggle to get things done. I live at a much slower pace than earlier in life.

Mental Illness

Psychological

"There is no normal life that is free of pain.
It's the very wrestling with our problems that can be the impetus for
our growth."

—FRED ROGERS[1]

WE'RE ALL LOOKING FOR something. For the hungry, it's the next meal. For those who are depressed, it's a glimmer of hope. For those neglected, it's to feel somewhat valued. Our searches can last a lifetime: for the right job, the right wife, the right vacation. And on, and on, 'til we breathe our last breath. Then, who knows?

My search for meaning became blocked at an early age. For whatever reason, I decided to try to end my life at age sixteen. Overdosing on a bottle of Bayer aspirin landed me in the hospital. Then a short while later, I sliced my wrists. Obviously, I was going in the wrong direction. My distracted, teenage mind could not wrap itself around the concept of God, which my weekly church attendance was supposed to inspire within me. As I will describe in more detail in the next chapter, *Social*, I didn't feel that I was living in a nurturing home environment; instead, I struggled daily to survive in what was an emotionally and physically violent

1. Rogers, *World According to Mister Rogers*, 112.

atmosphere. Without peace and goodwill between family members it was impossible for me to complete schoolwork or grow emotionally. I was blocked in more ways than one primarily because I did not feel valued. And without feeling valued, there was no progress forward.

A child, when undervalued and neglected will not flourish. And as such, I did not know why I existed. My goals were to escape the world I was forced to endure. One of my siblings was especially violent and tried in several instances, to murder me. Once, I was threatened at knife point, then shoved down a flight of stairs. I barely escaped and had some broken bones. "No one can control him," my dad told me. They put him in the psychiatric hospital for a time and a special class at school.

The religious people of a local church were not available to help me. I, personally, didn't know any church member who would intervene. I asked two neighborhood couples if I could live with them but they declined. I found no escape until at the age of eighteen a quasi-religious cult swept me off my feet on the college campus. I joined the Unification Church who worshipped an idol, the cult founder, the Reverend Sun Myung Moon. Moon claimed to be the second Messiah and Christ.

At one point after months of brain-washing indoctrination and inter-state travel in a white van with belligerent and hostile cult leaders, I, along with other cult members in dozens of other identical white vans, were unloaded into the former New Yorker Hotel, recently acquired by the cult. Physical exhaustion from endless fundraising (selling candy and flowers door to door) with little sleep, I only sought rest. I found an upper floor room and isolated myself in the old, dusty, Manhattan structure.

Nearly starving, and without access to adequate food and water resources for several weeks, I prayed to Moon, the idol, and meditated constantly, sitting cross-legged on the floor. Losing all track of time including which day or night, I eventually reached the point of hearing a whispered voice outside of my head, going from ear to ear, faster and faster. I experienced supernatural events: in one instance, my entire body being lifted off the floor of the room and set back down. Hearing demons and devils that demanded that I throw myself out the window from this upper story, it took every ounce of strength to mentally withstand them. I was bombarded with chaotic voices shouting names, profanity, curses, and accusations—barking out orders mixed with the sounds of distant sirens and honking vehicles throughout the urban jungle below.

The psychotic episode lasted for about eighteen months while I was in the cult and resulted in mental, emotional, and physical exhaustion. The cumulation of years of family neglect, wrongful cult worship, and subsequent psychosis destroyed any last connection I might have had to the real world. I was totally broken and suffered a form of psychic death. Far from home, with only the bare minimum of necessities, I was totally devastated. But then, all of a sudden, miraculously, in the middle of everything and while still in New York, God reached out to me in a Voice in the rain. A sudden thunderstorm erupted one night, and as I stood looking out an open window I heard from within the downpour of rain a majestic life-giving Voice proclaiming: *Believe in Jesus Christ and you'll be saved!"* This, then, was the turning point, or one of many, in a process that led to recovery.

After a period of time, I left the cult and my mother had me begin treatment with Russell Noyes Jr., MD, then a professor of psychiatry at the University of Iowa. At the time I first came under his care as a patient I think I must have been about four years old emotionally and mentally. But we had in common an understanding of Christian teaching. However, without immediately adhering to God's message in the rain, I could not obtain a foothold on which to rebuild my own life, the life which had been broken.

The psychosis plummeted me into, among other things, a life of poverty. Poverty is a heavy burden and an almost insurmountable barrier to recovery for most mental patients. Being deprived of all value and worth psychologically, I also found myself at rock bottom materially; and at this point I needed to focus on obtaining the basic necessities. At this time of my life I was too mentally ill to apply for government benefits. I was not even aware they existed.

Other people applied for these benefits for me, on my behalf without me knowing, and these benefits kicked in, providing for some of my physical needs; but emotionally, spiritually, and specifically, intellectually, I was starving. Having always loved school, I was now without the mental stability to use my brain except in some periodic personal reading. And I was bored. As such, I really didn't know the meaning of this emptiness or my overall condition as a human being, e.g., what was my purpose? Did I have physical brain damage, too, to contend with? Going to nearby Bible study groups, I found I was ostracized there due to my psychiatric diagnosis which I freely told them about; people did not understand what I was going through. There was a lack of compassion. And I'm sure my physical appearance gave an impression of mental disability causing people to keep their distance. The isolation was excruciating which led to suicidal thoughts and gestures.

Because I had previously gone through a psychosis, I was also somewhat emotionally withdrawn which is a side-effect of psychosis. And I lacked social skills with which to make new friends. The social rejection from others, especially the church, made me depressed which caused everything to seem futile. The aftermath of being in the cult which lasted for several years was a feeling of despair. The experience of being in the cult had a negative effect on me and for many years this was difficult to shake or live with on a daily basis. Afterall, worshipping an idol was contrary to my natural self that was created to worship the true God. Again, people did not understand and I found little compassion. Along with this, because of the brainwashing techniques used by cult leaders, my brain felt scrambled and thought processes were confused so much that it was difficult to be rational or logical.

Yet, I was encouraged to work so I tried waitressing, worked in a laundry—you name it, I tried it— anything in the Help Wanted newspaper ads. But what did I earn money *for*? I felt like Sisyphus, the figure in Greek mythology who was punished by Zeus by being forced to roll an immense boulder up a hill only for it to roll down every time it neared the top, repeating this action for eternity.[2] I

2. Sisyphus, Wikipedia, para 1.

wondered what meaning can be found in mere physical survival, living hand to mouth, day in and day out, without a transcendent purpose? Why did I do these things? Like in the Greek story, I was rolling the boulder up the hill only to find it rolling back down again, over and over in repetition, day in and day out, and what was the meaning or value in that? I disagree with an author I eventually read, Camus, who concluded that such an empty activity, though meaningless, creates an existential happiness.[3] For me, it absolutely did not.

Camus was an atheist. He called his philosophy absurdism. He tried to figure out how to live with integrity in a world that he considered as without meaning. Eastern University's Professor of Philosophy, Phil Cary, says that in Dante's *Divine Comedy*, hell always means being trapped in some way . . . a total inability to progress toward a worthwhile goal. No one in hell is on a journey that leads somewhere . . . So, spiritually speaking, being stuck in aimless motion is really just another way of being stuck, precisely because it's not a journey that gets you somewhere.[4] [End of Phil Cary on hell]

One of the reasons I was confused was because I felt stuck, I could not make any progress; subsequently, the despair and depression seemed endless. Even though I worked hard, I still lacked adequate food and clothing no matter how many hours I put in; and I lacked social support. Only qualifying for entry-level employment positions with little or no intellectual challenges, I was also extremely bored.

Another fraudulent area of my early adult life was the issue of a moral compass. I was so caught up in mere physical survival that I forgot the Christian teaching in virtues. Because of extreme isolation and loneliness, I was desperate for companionship and got involved with some bad male characters. This severely hampered my spiritual and ethical development. Sexuality without the covenant of marriage will always end in disaster. These relationships

3. Camus, *Myth of Sisyphusr*, 123.
4. Cary, "Weight of Love," 15–36.

will always result in heartbreak, and are a detour, leading us away from God, our supreme Good.

By the time I reached the age of thirty-nine, also afflicted now with the personality flaw involving impatience, I decided I'd had enough. Exhausted from my efforts to make a better life, and without one iota of hope, I thought it was time to quit trying. In addition, no human relationship had satisfied my longings for companionship and when one such romance turned bitter that was the last straw. Totally abandoned by all human contact now except for the limited and fragile ties within the medical field of psychiatry, there was absolutely nothing left to stop me from trying to end my life—my impulsiveness brought me to the brink.

But God had a different plan. And in the second section of this book, *Recovery*, I will elaborate on that.

Each person with a mental illness may have some or all of these psychological elements mentioned in this chapter. My own experience is not altogether unique. Human nature most likely contains universal elements that exist in every culture though manifested in different ways; and they can go wrong in various ways and in different combinations with the complication of each element influencing one another, back and forth through interaction. It cannot be over-stated that poverty with difficult living conditions is a major factor in how one feels, and this is a huge influence on the quality of day-to-day existence. Obviously, if a person lacks the basic necessities little else matters and most hours of the day are devoted to alleviating this condition.

Mental Illness

Social

"Enter Through the Back Door"

THE PSYCHOLOGICAL EFFECTS OF stigma dehumanize not only the targets of the abuse; but also dehumanizes the abusers. In a downtown mall location, I see a sign placed at the back door of a drop-in medical clinic: *Psychiatric Patients Enter Here*. This is reminiscent of the 1950s deep south social conditions for the Blacks: *Negroes Use Back Door*. Going around to the front of the clinic, I see a sign: *Psychiatric Patients Use Back Door*. Not only is this insulting; it denies the innate dignity and inherent worth of the mentally ill who are human beings just as much as other people. It degrades them, humiliates them, and makes them feel ostracized and outcast.

The psychological effects on me every time I walk by this sign is depressing. In twenty-first-century USA this should not be happening. Such cruel and inhumane attitudes toward the mentally ill is still in the dark ages. How will minds and hearts ever be changed? Hasn't there been any progress? With all the technological progress we see in modern society, are social conditions still so backward and barbaric? It appears so.

For too long, the mental patient, often of lower-income, has been abused and treated as less than human.

For too long, the mentally ill, the poor, are shoved aside from the mainstream.

For too long, the mentally ill, those silenced, are not heard: their cries, ignored, as the well-to-do, the comfortable, and posh rest in ease in their luxurious lifestyles and privileges. The respected ones do not wish to associate with the down-trodden. They are too busy with their travels and complacent pleasure-seeking vacations, to notice others without such comforts. In ritzy resorts and high-end hotels, there, a buffer protects them from the unsightly homeless mentally ill sitting on the sidewalk begging, who needs a second chance, and an opportunity to get back on their feet again.

Housing shortages, demolition of low-income units to make way for luxury condos, is the norm in the United States. Personally, I was denied a continuance of my lease several years ago because the owner planned to renovate my apartment for the well-to-do. My only choice was to move across town into a high-crime neighborhood where I encountered threats for my personal safety on a regular basis, predators everywhere, including hostile next-door tenants.

Having a place to live where you do not feel threatened is a major component in sound mental health. For part of my adult years, I lived in dangerous neighborhoods where predators were always a threat. As I mentioned in *Section One, Psychological*, when growing up, my home environment was horrific. I have learned from experience and subsequent research, that when a young teenage girl back in the 1960–70s who suffered from abuse in the home, left the home, and went out into the city, there was, literally, no one to offer refuge—no organization, no person—who would provide assistance. At the time I was desperate and my high school guidance counselor did not offer any solutions. She just told me to keep trying to do my school work so I could graduate and my plan to enter the Peace Core after graduation wasn't feasible due to my emotional problems. A young married couple in another building in the apartment complex where I lived with my father and older brother seemed friendly, so I asked them if I could move in with them. Of course, they said, "No, sorry." On another occasion, I went to the ER in the middle of the night with sliced, bloody wrists only to be rebuked by a harsh and judgmental nurse who offered no consolation or solutions as she slapped on bandages and sent me back home.

At seventeen years of age with no employment skills I faced insurmountable obstacles to independence. Doing school work was almost impossible due to my emotional problems and home environment. Depressed, semi-psychotic, and socially isolated, my world was caving in. It was no surprise, then, when a quasi-religious cult recruited me into their shady organization nine months after graduation from high school. I had attempted college classes and only completed a course in studio art. The cult people approached me on the college campus and bombarded me with attention. I was duped into thinking that they actually liked me. My cult experience which proceeded over the course of about three and a half years was a primary factor in my psychotic break which lasted about eighteen months. Then I escaped the cult and was hospitalized in Iowa City.

Social isolation, then, is a strong risk factor for mental illness, leaving a person vulnerable to dangerous organizations. If growing children and teens do not have the time and attention of good, supportive family members chances for survival are nil. If there is no other person outside the family who believes in supporting them, they will fall by the wayside and probably end up homeless. But this is not new; it has been known for centuries. So, why then, is it not appreciated more by some parents, teachers, and friends? We live in a modern world where priorities direct our attentions elsewhere. Economic insecurities deflect our energies from the goals of character development and support of the young. Who will teach the children basic survival skills, along with spiritual values and good morals? Who will teach the young to be loving and kind to their siblings and a good friend to others? How can we create a society where people look out for one another, our neighbors and friends, emotionally and economically?

As my life progressed after I left the cult and then through my adulthood, social problems continued to plague me. Continuing conflicts with relatives, involvement with bad characters in the surrounding community, employment failures—there seemed to be no end in sight. As I mentioned, at thirty-nine years of age I decided to give up and overdosed on medication. At the last minute I barely made it to a hospital emergency room where I immediately blacked out and fell down. It is clear that only God's intervention saved me from an untimely death.

As time went on living in low-income housing brought more challenges because apartments are dwellings where complete strangers of either gender live in close proximity. Not everyone has a kind heart or behaves in a civil manner. Some are overtly hostile, power-hungry, and predatory. There is criminal behavior: drug dealers, prostitution, stalking. And one next door neighbor pounded on walls and banged cupboards. Both she and others on many occasions violently and loudly, slam their doors, which is very disturbing for me. Social environments which are so combative and disruptive affect our mental health greatly and contribute to on-going emotional problems.

Even though I often crave companionship, my need for time alone is stronger. There is a mental problem that long conversations with friends mess up my mind. I cannot tolerate long interactions with others. Some periods of isolation are conducive for a writer who has to be alone to get some work done. My best time for writing is between mid-night and 4am, in the still of the darkest night.

Mental Illness

Spiritual

For our struggle is not against flesh and blood,
but against the rulers, against the authorities,
against the powers of this dark world and
against the spiritual forces of evil in the heavenly realms.

Ephesians 6:12 NIV

There will always be spiritual battles for as long as we live; and this is not unique for those with mental illness alone. All humans fight them whether they acknowledge it or not. Identifying them as such gives a person an advantage because when they are ignored, a person can be controlled by the unseen. This is from a biblical perspective.

I think my first encounters with what I describe as a spiritual battle began when I was just a small child, sometime before the age of seven, I'm not sure of the exact age. On one occasion, I remember lying in bed in the dark night and hearing what I thought were evil witches in the attic, maybe three of them. There was a small boarded opening in the ceiling that opened to the attic and even though it was closed I could hear the witches who were just beyond that, laughing and carrying on. It alarmed me; but eventually, I just went to sleep.

On another occasion when I was about five or six, it occurred to me to walk down our back alley behind my family's house. This was a time in 1950s America when neighborhoods had rows of houses lining the streets with alleyways between the rows of houses which would allow automobiles to gain access to garages from the rear. So, one day, I started walking down the alley, a dusty, gravel road, and went quite a distance. It was a gray, cloudy afternoon and I, suddenly, without provocation, became afraid of flying monkeys that were going to swoop down any second using their wings, and attack me with their sharp claws. I ran for my life, looking back over my shoulder periodically, to escape. With relief, I finally made it to my family's house and once inside, closed the door very securely. I don't believe I told anyone.

Once past the age of ten, my spiritual battles continued only now mostly involving humans. Since people are spiritual beings, I call these conflicts spiritual battles as well. A female neighborhood schoolmate decided to beat me up because I said I didn't like Elvis. She was a Tomboy and had me on the ground, beating me with her fists. Battles also with males during elementary school age were a regular experience, spiritual conflict with boys who seemed to enjoy tormenting me by name calling.

Spiritual battles became very severe when I was in the cult, as I've mentioned, during the psychotic break of 1976. Not many people will admit that the devil is a real entity with all his minions; but for me, it changed my life dramatically. Few can argue with real life experience. The mental patient is the expert, not an outside observer. Few mentally ill have the platform on which to assert their opinions. Much of the experience a mentally ill person has is silenced and the ill are oppressed by those who wish to impose their own materialistic worldview or perspective. My worldview incorporates the spiritual realm along with the physical; and within this spiritual realm are dark, evil forces which strive to separate us from the love of God and his saving grace. These forces congregate in certain locations and attack in patterns. Emotional and psychological well-being is disrupted in the person who is attacked.

The demonic voices in my psychotic break had as their source evil beings with an intelligence. They connived to make my life uncomfortable (to put it mildly). They were in the room I was in, or flew around my head. Some people who have lived around me were influenced by the demonic or were partially possessed by them. These people have had the goal of disturbing me with the aim of making me lose my faith in God and to lose all hope for the future. There is an emotional darkness, a spiritual blockage. All hope of a better life is destroyed. This is what the dark forces want with the ultimate goal of convincing people to commit suicide. Some succumb to chain smoking. Some become alcoholics. Some, compulsive eaters. I smoked for a while at the time of doing some volunteer work to try to fit in with other people who smoked; but I did not get addicted and was able to quit after a short period of time. For a while I did try to comfort myself with a type of compulsive eating but was able to curb that. I did not turn to alcohol. Some people resort to immoral lifestyles with sexual promiscuity, illicit drug use, and other unethical conduct. These types of behaviors have a negative spiritual component that will take a person further and further away from God because sin separates us from God. God is the source of life and energy and wholeness. Substitutionary behaviors will end in failure and are harmful to mental health. I got involved in some relationships that were harmful mostly because I told myself that what I was looking for was actually a husband.

Without a strong connection to a religious body I suffered, personally, with a weak faith and I also, at times, found life meaningless. I attended college off and on but could not stick with anything. Afterall, what was I studying *for*? Did I have any long-term goals—something to live for? For several years after leaving the cult I had become focused on what the surrounding culture said was important: physical attractiveness, romance, status. I focused mainly on myself, exercising, sunbathing, shopping. I married a Yale graduate, but it soon ended in divorce. While together, we visited several Art Museums or Institutes within a 300-mile radius. I tried to explore new cooking skills and bought a wok. We got cats for pets. Still, my empty life had an existential vacuum in it;[1] and the symptoms from my schizophrenic disorder also did not abate. I was on the early generation of meds which were pretty much ineffective; and, still, on occasion, heard what I coined *evil spirit music.*

A major spiritual problem I've had and which has been magnified in recent years, is my inability to tolerate heat. It took a while for me to gain this insight. Whether it is in my apartment or outdoors, when I'm walking down the street to go to the pharmacy or a store, my mental state changes and I become bombarded with a hell of demonic thoughts. Accusations fill my mind of those I normally love, swear words, profanity—you name it—hateful words go against me and others. The temperature may be in the seventies or eighties with bright sunshine or sometimes in the nineties with heat indexes in the hundreds, and as I walk along, I'm enduring my own personal hell of a mental state. When I'm able to return to an air-conditioned environment once again, this bombardment abates but not without repercussions. I'm left in a kind of shock for what I had to endure. Eventually, I can return to normal or what I consider normal for me.

While searching for a way to survive immediately after leaving the cult, I left out regular prayer and did not seek God's guidance for the day. My parents had taken away my Bible. I also did not seek God's help during moments of crisis. My mental life was one of confusion and I was unprotected spiritually and emotionally. In retrospect, I believe it's a wonder I survived at all.

---

1. Frankl, *Man's Search*, 106–8, 141.

II

RECOVERY

Recovery
Biological

But he said to me, "My grace is sufficient for you,
for my power is made perfect in weakness."

2 COR 12:9 ESV

IN MY RELIGION, THERE is a teaching for how weakness can be used for good: For we do not want you to be unaware, brothers, of the affliction we experienced in Asia. For we were so utterly burdened beyond our strength that we despaired of life itself. Indeed, we felt that we had received the sentence of death. *But that was to make us rely not on ourselves but on God* who raises the dead. He delivered us from such a deadly peril, and he will deliver us. On him we have set our hope that he will deliver us again. (2Cor 1:8-10 ESV, emphasis author's)

Modern day psychiatry has offered medication as an answer to mental illness. I believe that, often, medications can help a person who has schizophrenia or a psychotic illness. It took a lot of trial and errors, but my doctors finally settled on prescribing Risperdal and its generic, risperidone, for my schizophrenia. This seems to help, and cushions me from an over-stimulating surrounding social environment; but I believe that it also helps to shelter me from hallucinations, at least part of the time. I still have some residual symptoms. As far as major depression, we've tried several anti-depressants but I was unable to tolerate the side effects. In addition, I prefer to get at the root of what is making me sad and find the cause of my hopelessness which is a spiritual and psychological problem.

I mentioned the addiction I believe I had with diet pop in Section One. My use of coffee for the caffeine has become necessary whenever I start my day, have had paid employment or did volunteer work. However, my energy level has sometimes become so low that, sometimes, I can barely stand or walk.

I only discovered crisis center food banks when I reached my fifties. They have supplied some of my food when I run out of funds every mid-month. In the past I could walk to a couple of church-sponsored food banks in my neighborhood or have them deliver. Friends, sometimes, drove me to the food banks which was a big help. I have made efforts to eat healthy. I taught myself how to cook, especially soups and legume or vegetable dishes which are inexpensive. I usually carry a peanut butter sandwich or a bag of peanuts in my backpack at all times, along with a bottle of juice. This not only helps when I get low blood sugar, but saves money from avoiding the purchase of snacks. I'm grateful for all the friends who have assisted me in finding food resources or who donated some to me. Church friends have, at times, given me vegetables grown in the church garden. Without the assistance of the food banks and friends I, literally, would not have survived.

To try to strengthen myself, I've used swimming and other exercise at a local pool. During a period of relatively good health in my thirties and fifties, I would go four or five times a week and swim laps for about thirty minutes at a time. The city gives a discount for the swim pass to low-income citizens. And since I've never owned a vehicle, I've walked more than most people I know. This is in addition to taking mass transit.

In Section One I mentioned my unpleasant housing situation. So, what did I do to improve my housing situation? To improve my lot over the years I have played by the rules, never got evicted, and nearly always paid my rent on time. My government housing worker told me toward the end of our working relationship that I had been a *stellar* client. I have to add that she has been a remarkable and steadfast helper over a period of several decades whom I will always be grateful to. I have applied for a unit in a nicer complex in a better location where the building's potential tenants are meticulously screened. This is a clean building which is well maintained and has security. From those I've met, fellow tenants there are well-mannered and civil.

My friends and a distant relative have also provided clothing for me. Occasionally, they have given me boxes or bags full of used or new clothes. Otherwise, it would have been difficult for me to obtain these items. For a while, a relative helped me to get new shoes; now I have orthopedic shoes which are covered by my insurance.

I use two crutches. I own a wheelchair. My lower limbs are in pain and are weak. The medical field has not yet found a source of this problem even after many tests. At the time of this writing, I have applied for a wheelchair accessible apartment unit.

Finding myself completely without resources early in life— actually, destitute—by the time I am in my senior years I have found that God eventually provided for all my needs. Over the course of my lifetime, it has become evident that as a physically and mentally disabled adult I am totally dependent on God and Christians and other good people in the surrounding community. I am weak, but God (and his people), are strong. Survival depends upon God's provision. Without familial ties and support, a disabled human being has little chance to survive in our modern world. In my situation it was largely, with a few exceptions, individual Christians and other altruistic people from within the civic community who supported me; and because of this I am able to survive and carry out my writing and advocacy work.

Recovery

Psychological

Teachable—1a: capable of being taught;
b: apt and willing to learn[1]

THE FUNDAMENTAL PRINCIPLE IN psychological recovery from mental illness is the willingness of the patient to learn, who has the capability of being taught. Without this, all else fails. I cannot stress this enough. In order to learn a person needs, first and foremost, an attitude of humility, the idea that one doesn't know everything, and perhaps, another person might be smarter than herself/himself or at least have something to offer, be it an author, instructor, mentor, etc. And curiosity doesn't hurt; the search for answers helps. If a person loses all their motivation for these things, stagnancy sets in with the danger of sinking deeper and deeper into various pathologies where mental states will eventually degenerate into a point of no return. This needs to be avoided at all costs. Learning is the foundation upon which all recovery is built. A prudent health care provider will recognize this and model such characteristics for the patient, thus encouraging psychological growth leading to more successful outcomes. Being goal oriented and *teachable*, to learn, one must have a good attitude, an

1. Merriam-Webster, *definition*, para 1.

openness to what is new, different, and advantageous, as well as the belief that it will do some good.

There are different kinds of learning. According to author and speaker, Malcolm Gladwell, *capitalization learning* is when we get good at something by building on the strengths that we are naturally given [were born with] and this is relatively easy.[2] However, when there is no choice in the matter because we face difficulties in life, then we build upon our strengths and this is called *compensation learning*—a person has to focus hard to succeed and it takes great effort.[3] Gladwell states that when a person has a disability, the learning of new skills and lessons are done in a more powerful way because of the obstacles that had to be overcome. Necessity, therefore, has the favorable result of more powerful learning and strength of lessons because of the extra effort put in than if the task had been simple to do.[4]

Those who have considerable obstacles to overcome are usually more motivated to succeed, *unless*, and it is a significant unless, the obstacles are too numerous or severe—which will vary for each individual's tolerance level. Sometimes, people are crushed by hardships; other times, they will overcome and be victorious. In my previous work, *Reflections on the Meaning of Mental Integrity*, I gave real-life contrasting examples of, first, a pampered, spoiled person from a wealthy family, who had everything simply given to him his entire life, but then who ended up an unemployable drug addict. And someone who was brought up in more modest circumstances who had a religious upbringing instilled, with a strong work ethic, who internalized moral standards which gave him the impetus to persevere and, ultimately, to overcome significant obstacles and succeed.[5]

As a person who's had significant obstacles to overcome, myself, what did I need to learn to recover from serious mental illness? And what meaning has serious mental illness had for me?

2. Gladwell, *David and Goliath*, 112–13.

3. Gladwell, *David and Goliath*, 112–13.

4. Gladwell, *David and Goliath*, 112–13.

5. Murphy, *Reflections Mental Integrity*, 39.

For one thing, I have sought healing and to obtain good health and wholeness or integrity. I have wanted to be rid of all psychiatric symptoms and rejoin the *normal world*. I have striven to my utmost ability to follow doctors' orders and have acquiesced at times, after questioning treatments. However, with certain medications—which had deleterious side effects—I did have to protest and I declined further treatment with these medications.

At one time in the US, the popular perspective on mental illness was that it is mostly biochemical. This is reductionistic and simplistic. Since my view of the human being is more holistic, it stands to reason that we need multidisciplinary therapies to treat the whole person. We have psychology, theology, and science, with each contributing something worthwhile. If people ignore spirituality, as has been traditionally done in psychiatry, patients will only live in a mere survival mode. Religion can contribute the additional dimension of good ethical values or virtues and reasons to live. And when someone with mental illness reaches a consciousness of personal responsibility and awareness of an obligation to serve others in the broader community, this is a good outcome. Without consciously taking responsibility for various areas of life, recovery is unlikely. It takes personal insight to understand our own mental illness and to strive to improve the situation. How does one acquire insight? And what are we responsible for? For one: our own daily lifestyles and how we conduct ourselves, e.g., civility, trying to maintain good relationships, productivity, respect for people of diverse ethnic backgrounds; living justly on the planet and contributing something worthwhile for the benefit of others.

Many people with mental illness don't have insight about their mental state and can't sense a purpose for their lives so they just eat and sleep, smoke, do illicit drugs and alcohol, and engage in risky illicit sexual behaviors. The lack of good religious values leaves an existential vacuum[6] which has to be filled; and this is often done with these destructive elements which degenerate the psyche into further realms of madness. Good values in conjunction with healthy lifestyles are essential for recovery. In the

---

6. Frankl, *Man's Search*, 106–8, 141.

twenty-first century, psychiatric care providers are beginning to recognize this and are steering psychotherapy into the realm of values. However, in the last forty years when government entities sliced mental health programs' budgets, the options for diverse wholistic treatments dwindled. When patients can't form healthy lifestyles for themselves this contributes to bad mental health. Unfortunately, we have seen many of them when in crisis mode given only thirty minutes in the ER and then tossed out. The shelters are over-crowded and overwhelmed, so many are turned away. All these problems magnify and compound the desperate situation of the mentally ill.

When I entered the psychiatric world during the 1970s, the biological revolution was in full force, at least in the Midwestern part of the country. Fortunately, I have had psychiatrists and one psychologist who also see the value of religion as another factor in good mental health. Overall, the psychiatric field has been good to me and I am grateful for the patience, endurance, and perseverance many of my providers showed. I have not always been an easy patient to take care of; but then, occasionally, the providers, themselves, were also a bit difficult. We're all in this together, so forgiveness is in order all around. My illness has brought many intelligent and highly educated professionals into my life that I would not have ordinarily encountered had I not been ill. They have modeled some good characteristics. Knowing these individuals has been helpful on my life's difficult journey which would have taken a very different direction had I not known them.

As I mentioned in other parts of this booklet, poverty has been a major obstacle which has been a big challenge psychologically and physically. When you don't know if you will have enough food to get through the month, this disruption hinders the accomplishment of other worthy goals. Human flourishing involves a lot more than merely eating and drinking; indeed, that would be hardly above the animal level of existence. A human being needs to do more than merely survive. I needed to believe that I had a future and could set goals. I was given the gift or talent of writing. This is something that came easily to me in my youth and as I matured. There must have been some reason I was born with this talent, sort of a God-given mission. I was given a task. What has been the mission of my writing? I believe it is to share the basic message of reconciliation with God. People, and in my case, the mentally ill, need to be reconciled to God; and the prerequisite for this is realizing our dependence on God.

Being mentally ill is a brain disorder but also is about being out of harmony with God and the world. It is physically, having a brain and thinking disorder which spills over into disorder socially, and, ultimately, spiritually. Not having good mental health creates havoc in all areas of our lives with lifestyles and negative behaviors which ultimately result in ruin. To get on track with good mental health, along with psychiatric treatments, an individual needs to acknowledge God and dependence on this God who is the great healer. Even though this will not solve all our problems, we can be confident that God will help us through the hard times.

Since I've had personal experience with mental illness, I believe I have had a responsibility to write articles and books to share my experience and provide insights and lessons I've learned over the course of my life. If this writing has prevented some suffering or improved the lives of others, then that is a good thing. My attitude during recovery is one of striving to become a better human being, i.e., more compassionate, giving, thoughtful. As I mentioned, education is paramount in recovery, learning more about subjects pertaining to health, both physical and mental. I have fed my curiosity about numerous subjects and sought to develop my talents.

Along with writing, for a number of years I was a public speaker. Sharing my story has been meaningful, though, at times, difficult. I'm not a natural speaker, so it was difficult to share my story in that manner. Along with these activities, I've done advocacy work for the mentally ill through various projects, one being that I set up a fund to help low-income psychiatric patients with clothing and other items at our state hospital. It has felt natural to do these things since I made connections at the hospital through my many years of volunteer work. Advocating for the mentally ill in practical ways has also turned out to be a fulfilling activity for me.

How have I been able to find this meaning and what has it meant in terms of recovery? First off, my trial of psychosis while in the cult and, subsequently, the effects of schizophrenia and major depression, left me with the feeling of *anhedonia* which is defined as the loss of pleasure or lack of reactivity to pleasurable stimuli.[7] I could not feel any emotions, lost interest in daily activities such as socializing and any kind of work, and could not figure out any reasons as to why I should live. A big problem was a lack of motivation due to numbness, deadness of spirit, and lack of pleasure in normal daily activities. So, what turned this situation around? What was it that changed so that I could find meaning and purpose? I needed to find that I had a future and could set goals beyond merely to survive a particular day. In doing what follows I was able to gain back some emotions and feelings, an interest in life again; the numbness and deadness of spirit became less.

My nature is to fight for what's right, to argue in a polemical way to defend the truth. My name is Marcia. At *Meaning of the Name,*[8] Marcia is Latin for dedicated to Mars, the Roman god of war. Having to fight for my sanity all my life and to struggle for physical survival was only part of the problem. I found that I have also needed to continuously defend the Gospel within the religious sphere. There have been pastors in various denominations who preach that there are other ways to God besides Christ, and they are doing this in what are labeled Christian churches. But I believe in this scriptural verse: *For there is one God and one mediator between God and mankind, the man Christ Jesus, who gave himself as a ransom for all people.* (1 Tim 2:5–6a ESV)

I have been a member of or have visited several churches besides the Presbyterian Church USA, e.g., Lutheran ELCA, Roman Catholic, Christ of Christ, Baptist, Church of the Nazarene. One pastor said, "What you believe doesn't matter; just be loving." That is ludicrous. His ministry was cut short by his untimely death.

---

7. Pizzagalli, "Better Understanding," line 1–2a.

8. Meaning of the Name, "Meaning of the Name Marcia," para 3.

Another pastor said that Christ was a sinful man up to the point of being nailed to the cross, and at the point of crucifixion Christ became divine. One pastor said that John the Baptist was Jesus's mentor. I heard all this and other such nonsense. My authority for the eternal divinity of Christ as the Word is found in scripture; Christ existed in relationship with the Father and Holy Spirit throughout all eternity: *In the beginning was the Word, and the Word was with God, and the Word was God. He was in the beginning with God. All things were made through him, and without him was not anything made that was made.* (John 1:1–3 ESV)

One church member called me a *Fundamentalist!* with a derogatory tone of voice, sort accusing me for doing something wrong. Why? Because I said that I believe in the Gospel of John in the Bible, that it was true. We were involved in a church Bible study group, but horrors! if you actually believe that the Bible had some truth in it. *Gasp.* Sometimes, when sitting in unorthodox worship services I have felt extreme chest pain as false assertions were made about Christ; I felt like I was having a heart attack and I couldn't breathe for a few seconds as my hands clasped at my chest. Melodramatic? Maybe, but it really happened.

I support the social justice movements for various causes and also believe in social inclusion for all the different types of people, both convictions of which typically come from the ideological left; but at the same time, I also have very traditional theological views and the unorthodox ideas promoted by some clergy motivated me to write a rebuttal. See my essay, *Christian Apologetics and Postmodernism: A Rebuttal,* posted at my website (Hopeforrecovery. com) or in my book: *The Collected Writings of Marcia A. Murphy, Christus Magnus Medicus Sanat (Christ, the Great Physician, Heals).*[9]

I have found meaning as an advocate; I've wanted to defend others who are afflicted with mental illness and poverty through my writing, speaking, and by on the ground, practical measures. Everything like this is a struggle because as we all know the world rewards the strong, rich, and prosperous—things I am not. I've

---

9. Murphy, *Collected Writings,* 51–60.

come up against forces in society which go in the opposite direction of myself. We could also include male/female power struggles but that is not within the scope of this current project. Here, I am confining my discussion to *meaning*.

When God talks to you, to not listen is the utmost in foolishness and a recipe for self-destruction. I was told that *Jesus Christ saves*. Saves us from what? Well, from the demons, for one. When I heard the Voice in the rain, I was being bombarded by all the demonic realm could muster. My spiritual life was on the line. I was, in a sense, doomed. My prayers and thoughts had to be redirected to God for his protection and saving grace. My survival depended on this very thing. God got my attention with the Voice in the rain and saved my soul.

To save my life further from meaninglessness and lack of purpose, God directed my thoughts daily on an on-going basis. People, places, and things inspired me to do this and that. To give you an example, I was encouraged by a psychiatrist to follow my heart in writing. He was unaware at the time that I had started to write as a young girl and teenager. I had always wanted to be a published author. So, when this psychiatrist agreed with me that I should tell my story, this was much needed support to carry it out. I could not have done all the writing I've accomplished over the many years without some encouragement. At one time I formed a writers' support group with two other ladies, both Mennonites. Another time, I joined the University Women's Writers' Group who also gave me invaluable feedback, support, and encouragement.

Another way I found meaning was to read books and articles, as many as I could possibly read. Topics included the connection between spirituality and health, primarily, mental health. I also studied topics such as philosophy, theology, and even physics. Mentors came into my life from various fields. I've also read about historical problems of the poor, especially, impoverished women in the 1800s. Mainly, with a few exceptions, my interests have been motivated by newly generated feelings; feelings of empathy for the afflicted and an effort to right wrongs.

There are always battles. Battles to obtain funding for projects, battles to acquire access at libraries, battles to assert ideas in a hostile ideological environment. Like my namesake, the war goddess of Mars, I will defend my rights and the rights of others. And there is resistance because, for one, I am female. Females have been, traditionally, kept in the home, in the kitchen, barefoot, and pregnant. I will remind the reader of many exceptions to this rule throughout history: Deborah, a judge and prophet of the Old Testament, see (Judges 4 ESV); Lydia, seller of purple cloth of the New Testament who was compelled to listen to Paul when he shared God's message, (Acts 16:14 ESV). Later on, there was Joan of Arc of France; and nineteenth and early twentieth century female leaders of the suffrage movement who worked to acquire the right to vote for women in the United States: activists Susan B. Anthony and Elizabeth Cady Stanton. Still, more determined women have come to the fore: Dorothy Day, co-founder with Peter Maurin of the Catholic Worker movement, devoted her life to serving the homeless of New York City. She was a tireless advocate for peace and justice in both word and deed.[10] The list could go on because not all females have lived a lifestyle of the typical homemaker, nurse, or teacher and, who, by choice, worked to make some real changes in the world.

To repeat, my meaning came in advocacy for the poor and mentally ill population through writing and projects related to lifting others up from destitution. But in order for me to do these things I first had to have enough food to eat, clothes to wear, and a decent place to live. God provided, and I am grateful for all the helpers who came along side of me throughout my life. Facing a lot of stigma, I've had to endure rejection, mistreatment, and exclusion. I've not been able to verbally defend myself on most occasions so I usually just walk away. For example, I've been treated rudely by store clerks that have a cruel tone of voice and rough manner with my groceries. This has happened a lot for many years. For some reason I must appear as a mentally ill person or of lower class because it provokes some reaction. My choice is whether I'll

10. Trinity Stores, *Dorothy Day*, para 1.

stop going to go the business establishment or I can try to forgive and keep going. Since I have transportation issues being with out a car, I go where the bus takes me and that leaves me with few alternatives as to where I'll shop. I usually keep going and hope and pray that the mean people will not be working that day; or I pray for God to bless them and to soften their hearts.

I touched upon the importance of lifestyles. Along with the ability to learn, which is important in a psychological recovery process is how a person structures their day. Is daily life meaningful? This would involve habits or patterns of living throughout the day. Repetition of activities we value will determine the quality of our lives. Some value pleasure while others seek power or wealth and these aims will ultimately result in frustration and lack of fulfillment. Humans were created to be in relationship with their Creator, so everything done during the day is to reflect this basic aim of seeking harmony with God, or else be in rebellion. Rebellion against God is futile and the sooner one finds this out the better.

We have tasks to do every day and tasks have a taskmaster. This does not cease when we reach our senior years as I have. Some people think that at the age of retirement you just sit back and lead a self-centered, vegetative, and complacent lifestyle. However, I believe that if you look around you, you will find plenty to do because of so many needs in the community being currently unmet. Feed the hungry, house the poor, clothe the naked, etc.; so much to do within our communities and the world. Jesus never instructed us to stop our work and just relax, sit back, and sip lemonade on a remote island's white, sandy beach. As long as people somewhere, someplace, are suffering, our work is never done; there is always a task before us. And these tasks keep us psychologically fit and healthy long into advanced years. We need to keep looking forward for more work to do.

Psychology and spirituality often overlap. *The Seven Deadly Sins*, by Jewish psychologist, Solomon Schimmel, has helped me to visualize the sinful nature, i.e., pride, anger, envy, greed, gluttony, lust, and sloth which, conversely, leads to contemplate the opposite, virtues, and morals. Having a real-life role model or someone to imitate has the potential to help us become more fully human and a better person overall. This would be on-going and promotes continuous development of good moral character throughout our entire lives.

Difficulties, coping, enduring, and finding solutions creatively can build character.

With character, comes hope.

Not only that, but we rejoice in our sufferings, knowing that suffering produces endurance, and endurance produces character, and character produces hope. (Rom 5:3–4 ESV)

Recovery

Social

If so many men, so many minds,
certainly, so many hearts, so many kinds of love.

—Leo Tolstoy

During my recovery process I found some therapists to be helpful. However, at times, I wrongfully substituted a therapist for the worship of God and following scripture. It was a matter of disordered loves, wrong priorities. People will sometimes put all their hopes and confidence in a therapist that should, first of all, be directed toward God. After loving God and doing his will— which involves obeying his commands—a person can then consider a therapist's advice.

People may think of various books as authoritative when, instead, holy scripture should be their ultimate and final truth for guidance. The same type of problem of disordered loves can develop with relationships with spouses. For example, I, for one, in the past, would idolize my partner or when married, my spouse. I did not have my ducks in proper order. I needed to love and respect God the most; and then the Bible; and other people and things, follows.

As I mentioned earlier, the social atmosphere of my apartment buildings I lived in caused psychological distress for me.

Neighbors in my apartment buildings posed, at times, a criminal threat which can be charged as either a misdemeanor or felony offense. Anyone convicted of making a criminal threat faces a substantial time in jail or prison. I reported such threats to my apartment managers; however, they did not stop the neighbors from acting in predatory ways. My solution was to move away to a new location; and since I needed a wheelchair or handicap accessible unit for my mobility issues, it was even more important for me to find a new home.

One deviation in my social recovery was my experience in my thirties while learning a martial art, Taekwondo, and the crush I had on one of my instructors, an Asian woman with a black belt (the highest ranking). Taekwondo, is a method of training and disciplining the body and mind. This was good exercise. Thankfully, my infatuation was not reciprocated and I only admired this instructor from afar. I now believe it was best to not to become involved. I don't believe same-sex romances are biblically sanctioned (Rom. 1:18–32 ESV) and I think they can be psychologically, unhealthy, as well as in some cases with males, physically injurious. I have a very traditional view of theology and relationships, and believe that marriage is between one man and one woman. Even though there are books out defending the LGBTQ+ lifestyle, and I have many friends who go along with them, it is my prerogative to believe what the Bible says about this matter, and my right as a free citizen to publish it.

When I've experienced conflicts with neighbors or if I don't like certain people, what do I do? I pray for them. As I've mentioned, I've also encountered a lot of obstacles from being rejected because of social stigma. What has been my attitude toward these obstacles in the social realm? Being rejected by various organizations, groups, as well as individuals, e.g., openly mocked and abused psychologically and physically; subject of gossip and a victim of backstabbing; being excluded—just about anything you can think of done to an outcast—this was a very powerful deterrent to forming friendships. Many times, I was completely discouraged from socializing. Ostracism can lead to aggression in those who are excluded because being excluded affects a person's mental health, in some cases, causing anger.[1]

Some people treat me as though I am a child. Is it because I am lower income? Or disabled? I am an adult in my late sixties (as I pen this); I am old enough to be someone's mother. Yet people treat me as though they are looking down on me. I believe that when a person is of lower income many people believe that the poverty-stricken are inferior human beings, who cannot think well, and who do not know how to behave. However, it is rather the reverse because anyone who looks down on another based on economics is the deviant one; for as it says in God's kingdom (where everything is reversed): *Blessed are you who are poor for yours is the kingdom of God.* (Luke 6:20 ESV) I am most comfortable in the company of the poor and outcast. They come across as unpretentious and they don't put on airs.

In order to function on a daily basis, I have learned to pray and ask God to fill me with forgiveness for the people who've mistreated and rejected me; and I ask God to bless my enemies. I have found that praying for people I don't like or who've mistreated me helps to put things into perspective and softens the blow. Forgiveness also has the power to open doors to the future. When I've found myself in a bitter, unforgiving frame of mind, making an effort to forgive people brings about inner peace with hope for a better future. But this can be especially difficult if I don't see an end to the mistreatment which is the case for the disabled. Finding comfort within the subculture then becomes paramount to endure such circumstances.

My closest friends are outcasts. I see them often when I go downtown, to libraries or coffee shops to work on my projects. The rejected ones know what it is like to feel humiliated, shunned, denigrated, all those things that destroy our dignity. We are embarrassed for not having dignity. We just want some peace. We discuss how to help the homeless, what sleeping quarters could be provided (perhaps some temporary bunk houses, separate quarters for males and females). We think creatively about how to

1. Denghao et al., "Ostracism Increases Aggression," para. 1.

provide jobs for the homeless so they can earn their shelter like using construction wood scraps to build birdhouses. But, of course,
for this you would need liability insurance, table saws, pick-up
trucks, nails and hammers. One friend said he could design the
building plans for the bird houses.

An important part of my social recovery, along with friendships with other outcasts, are my relationships with doctors; doctors by way of PhDs, MDs, and such. For some reason they have
been an important part of my life. Being overwhelmed by mental
illness, I have needed psychiatrists. Having Type 2 diabetes and
other physical illnesses or disorders, I have needed medical doctors and specialists. I've had surgeries and physical therapy, and
have needed medications on a long-term basis.

My relationships with several individuals who hold PhDs
were intrinsic to my building a good quality of life. I love to study.
I love sitting down with a good cup of coffee and focusing on some
reading to the exclusion of the outside world. My choice of topics
has varied over the years and with such variation came numerous
experts who've personally guided me, professors of history, Eng-
lish, philosophy, theology, music, law. These relationships helped
to activate and stimulate my intellectual development and educa-
tional growth. As I have only finished one year of formal college
education, these professors filled the void for needed instruction. I
am a life-long learner and I pray often for a teachable heart.

To be quite honest, my relationships with church people have
been a challenge. Some keep a big distance, physically, as well
as emotionally. Most do not have any previous experience with
someone with schizophrenia, so they are afraid of me. Or their
previous experience with someone with schizophrenia frightened
them; maybe the sick person was violent or aggressive. I want to
assure them that I am quite mild-mannered. I am more often a victim of aggression and less likely, a perpetrator. So, it takes patience
all around. It takes time for people to get to know one another
and some will take initiative, while others will never give me the
opportunity to get to know them.

My publications are in the church library (as well as public libraries). One member said she read one of them and it helped her to understand me more. She had previously been judgmental and was now full of remorse. I've given presentations for the church adult education classes which also helped to overcome some of the stigma in the church. Some members have stood up for me and advocated for my mental health ministry work, which has been helpful.

My writing (books, articles) and website allowed me to reach out to others. It helped to communicate my feelings and thoughts. A long time ago, I felt very isolated. There were few friends. The writing, besides being a meaningful activity of creating literature, broadened my social contacts, not only with professionals in the field of writing, but with the readers who come from all walks of life. A significant time of my life was when I talked about my life and books with nursing staff and medical students at the University of Iowa Hospitals and Clinics. I did talks for approximately twelve years. At this time, I simultaneously worked as a volunteer in the hospital's Patients' Library where I did many things, advancing to volunteer statistician before retiring. This interaction helped me to develop my social skills. At the late part of my life, in my fifties, I was finally learning how to talk to others and to be civil. I learned when to speak and when to be silent. The people I worked with did not always like me, so I had to deal with that. My religion taught me to turn the other cheek and to love my enemies. (Luke 6:29; Matt. 5:44 ESV) When I practiced these things that Christ taught, one co-worker, who, in the beginning acted like she hated me, later, became my friend.

I have a few close church friends of all ages. We get together for coffee and conversation. When my building's laundry machines break down, one will do my laundry at her house. Many times, they provide transportation. We celebrate birthdays and milestones. Since I live alone, the texting and emails with my friends help to alleviate loneliness. But it wasn't always like this. When I was in my twenties and thirties, I desperately wanted female friends. Now in my senior years that void is being filled.

Some of my closest friends sometimes come from the opposite side of the political spectrum. I've always voted as a Democrat because they support the housing and food programs I've needed to survive on. Without this help, I would have been out on the streets, homeless and starving. Yet, emotionally, I do not have barriers when it comes to friendship. A married couple who've always been staunch Republicans provided transportation for me to and from church for many years. I actually agree with many of their views and love them deeply. And someone who has been a part of the LGBTQ+ lifestyle became a close friend though I do not support that kind of lifestyle. We never discuss it. But his friendship has saved me from total isolation during the pandemic and I care about him deeply. The list goes on. My friends are from all walks of life. I try to not put up barriers. Humans can learn to relate to each other based on our humanness, and disregard the ideological problems, or, at least, negotiate around them.

So then, what has happened with my physical family? I live by the dictum: Don't look back; however, if you do, do try to forgive. I cannot socialize or have any contact with my younger brother because it causes me to have a severe psychological psychotic reaction of post-traumatic stress syndrome (PTSD). This is because of how he treated me in the past. He has never apologized for his behavior or shown any remorse. The last time I talked to him I told him that I forgive him and that maybe (as he is a churchgoer), we would see each other again in heaven. For now, on earth, I will keep my distance. The Bible teaches that in order for us to be forgiven by God, we must forgive all those who've wronged us. (Matt. 6:14 ESV)

I must also forgive the cult leaders who led me astray and brainwashed me into false beliefs and the stress of a psychotic break. I must forgive my relatives who neglected to support me in various ways over my many adult years. I must forgive my former abusive male romantic partners for the exploitation and emotional harm they caused while at the time I am remorseful for having gotten involved in the first place. I must forgive the government for its paltry benefits that have been barely enough to scrape by on and nearly left me starving.

Yes, there is a lot to forgive and, conversely, to be grateful for. Many people, over the years, be it housing workers, healthcare providers, or complete strangers, have had compassion on my situation of abject poverty, psychological distress, and social isolation. I must confess that more than once I've pestered someone by wanting to talk in emails when they've had a lot of other responsibilities demanded of them. I will always be grateful for their patience and tolerance of my intrusions.

Recovery

Spiritual

We don't measure God by what we are.
We measure ourselves by what God is.

—St. John of the Cross

MY FIRST LONG-TERM PSYCHIATRIST has expressed his opinion that what the psychiatric field labels my *psychotic break* when in the cult, was similar to when Jesus was in the desert wilderness and he heard the devil speaking, and talked back to him, verbally battling with him. (Matt. 4:1–11 ESV) The voices I heard then, when I was in New York City while in a desperate situation were at first the sounds of demons and devils. This was not just a period of seconds, minutes, or hours; rather, it was continuous for a number of months, to a total of approximately a year and a half. Only when hospitalized back in Iowa, did the quiet period begin.

The Voice within the downpour of torrential rain showers occurred one night during a thunderstorm which I've interpreted theologically as hearing God's voice. God, through the Holy Spirit, said: *Believe in Jesus Christ and you'll be saved!* This occurred at the time when the demons were attacking me in full force, terrifying me and causing deep distress. I had gotten little sleep or any kind of rest around the clock for the eighteen months during this psychotic episode. However, as soon as I could comprehend

God's message, and I reflected upon it for a period of time, my life's direction improved. Eventually, I emerged from the cult, and through medical care in Iowa City which included medication and psychotherapy, my mind began to heal. Returning to the church was helpful when I found transportation or the church was within walking distance. Christ said: "*But when the Helper comes, whom I will send to you from the Father, the Spirit of truth, who proceeds from the Father, he will bear witness about me.*" (John 15:26 ESV)

Not everyone believes that God speaks to us, audibly, in this modern age. But what they think doesn't matter to me. I know from experience what happened and the subsequent fruit shows that the tree of divine intervention was real. For we know the validity of a tree by its fruit. Even some Christians will deny that God will speak to us in contemporary times. But who are they to put limits on God's abilities, creativity, and power? Who are they to judge whether or not God ever talks to us humans? People, including Christians, do not have the authority to decide whether or not God will speak to us audibly, with a voice we can hear. As I mentioned, we know the truth of a tree by its fruit. There are many examples in the Bible of God speaking audibly to humans. Christopher C.H. Cook, Emeritus Professor of Durham University, in *Hearing Voices, Demonic and Divine: Scientific and Theological Perspectives*, states that human beings can and do experience hearing God's voice, an interpersonal communication and divine encounter. Cook's book has many examples.[1]

What has been the spiritual meaning of my psychosis? Sometimes, I wonder if my trials with mental illness have been beneficial for me, spiritually. Afterall, it says in the Bible: *It is good for me that I was afflicted, that I might learn your statutes.* (Psalm 119:71 ESV) Am I a better person because of it? The fruit of my psychosis was, among other things, that I came to realize that I needed God in order to survive; I was dependent on God. Through prayer, scripture reading, and religious worship, I was able to turn my life around from one of severe mental illness to living out a process of recovery. Today, you can see severely mentally ill individuals

1. Cook, *Hearing Voices.*

walking around aimlessly in stores or on the streets talking out loud to themselves or invisible entities. Their condition deteriorates to the point of extreme sickness and to the point where you wonder how they can manage to function at all. I believe I was able to avoid this end because I heeded God's guidance from the Voice of the rain and started to make healthy choices.

There were three major determinants, all intertwined, that resulted in better spiritual health: the interactions with a mental health professional in psychotherapy which included treatments such as therapy and medications; church worship service attendance; and my own devotional times in my home that involves scripture reading and prayer. Having known the evil spirits or demons in what sounded like the very reality of hell itself, the Lord steered me away from this dark realm and into the kingdom of light. If it weren't for this—God's saving grace—I would have been literally dead long ago: spiritually dead by being cut off from God; and/or physically dead from starvation and exposure to the outdoor elements while being homeless.

After the nearly successful suicide attempt at the age of thirty-nine, how did I turn to God and a healthy direction? Was it gradual or through an abrupt decision? I must say that all my life, ever since I was a small child, weekly church attendance and the major religious holidays were important to me. Between the age of two and three I would constantly ask my mother if it was time to go to church. I loved church. I loved everything about it. It was heaven for me. This is something I've never lost. Even though I sometimes wandered away, got mixed up in a cult, it was a quasi-religious cult where we constantly talked about God. Only the cult's theology was wrong (Sun Myung Moon, the leader, said he was a perfect person and the Christ); and the cult's primary motive was to make a lot of money through the followers' efforts at fundraising (selling flowers, candles, candies). The cult still exists even today with businesses as fronts.

As I've described in my previous writing, not having transportation to enable me to get to churches was a big problem. And I suffered greatly because of it. Being cut off was more than physically not being able to get to the church building. I really needed the powerful worship services and connection to God's people. But I still had my faith. At one point in my thirties, I set up an altar in my livingroom. On the altar, I placed photos of Mother Teresa, lit candles, a Bible, and a cross. I prayed daily. I read about everything I could find either about Mother Teresa or things she had written, herself.

I listened to Christian music, including Christian radio stations and would sing along with them. I watched Christian TV shows and preachers. My love for God was strong. I had never turned my back on God though there were short periods of distractions. Socially, my relationships with males became so problematic that it distracted me from Christianity. For example, I joined a Unitarian Universalist Church which is not Christian; but soon left that for a strong (traditional) Roman Catholic Church which had weekday Mass. I loved going to Mass. Then, when I eventually moved across town, I could not worship with the Catholics on Sunday mornings because I still didn't own a car. When I was recovering from the suicide attempt at age thirty-nine, I reflected on my experience in the cult of the Voice in the rain and then realized I could just walk the three blocks down the street to attend a Presbyterian church. Though I didn't know anyone there, I thought I give it a try. After participating there for about two years as a visitor, I became a formal member.

Having relations with Christian communities helped restore me over a period of time from the condition of a completely broken and destroyed human being to relatively good health. It took many years, but God is patient, and the church is too. I am grateful. The Christian community is the kingdom of light; I could feel the difference, spiritually, on the day I officially committed myself to becoming a church member at the Presbyterian church.

Recovering from serious mental illness, spiritually, there is the opportunity to develop a heart (mind) of wisdom. Without this, it is easy to fail in many respects. So, how does one acquire wisdom? Ask God. *If any of you lacks wisdom, let him ask God, who gives generously to all without reproach, and it will be*

47

given him. But let him ask in faith, with no doubting, for the one who doubts is like a wave of the sea that is driven and tossed by the wind. (James 1:5–6 ESV)

Timothy Keller, DMin., author, and Pastor Emeritus, Redeemer Presbyterian Church, New York City, and his spouse, Kathy Keller, state that we can learn wisdom by experience plus taking the time for thought, reflection, and contemplation upon the experience.[2] They say that we also gain wisdom by studying the Word of God, and listening to the advice of mentors, other advisors, and friends.[3] I once heard a pastor say that reading a book is a spiritual activity. I agree. The Bible, as God's word, is especially spiritual because we are transformed and made new by reading scripture. Many years ago when I got brainwashed by the pseudo-religious cult I was in, my brain was actually damaged pretty radically. I was crippled intellectually by the psychotic episode, and could not think very well. As I started back into society in my twenties, I took up whatever was around me to try to rebuild my ability to read and to think well. At first, my Bible was taken away from me, so then I found Newsweek and Time magazine in an apartment community room which led me to check out books at our local public library.

In retrospect, I think that before I started reading the Bible on a regular basis, my values and lifestyle seemed atheistic or materialistic, hardly different than the surrounding secular culture. My problems kept getting worse, socially, economically, and physical health. Some of my behavior showed a lack of morals. I think this is true for many young and old people alike. I believe that many major problems in this country (US) arise from very few people reading scripture, i.e., the Bible. Research has shown that when a person reads the Bible four days a week or more, they have much less immoral behavior. When reading the Bible less than four times a week, (or not at all), they live lives similar to atheists behaviorally.[4] My morning devotions with Bible reading has been

2. Keller, Keller, *God's Wisdom*, 20.
3. Keller, Keller, *God's Wisdom*, 24.
4. Cole and Ovwigho, *Understanding the Bible*, 2.

an invaluable asset to my mental health and decision-making. I know that it is not popular nowadays to say we battle sin; however, this problem is very real for everyone and is one of the causes of unhappy lives. Uncontrollable sin holds many of us captive and we need to be set free.

I asked Phil Cary, his opinion on the topic of grace and how to gain free will and to be set free from sin. I said to him: You mentioned to me that Augustine, as well as, Calvin, and Luther, all believed that we need to pray and ask God for grace to be free from sin. The less sinful we are by the grace of God, the more freedom of will. Is this correct?

Phil Cary: Right. The sequence in Augustine's theology is: first (before we do anything about it) God gives grace, then we pray for more grace, as a result of which we are gradually freed from sin, which means our will becomes free, i.e., we learn to love God and neighbor, which leads in the end to both our neighbors and ourselves finding eternal happiness with God.[5] [End of Phil Cary on sin and grace, free will]

I have questioned whether or not I've learned anything over the years, if I've gained in wisdom during my recovery. I asked Phil Cary for what he saw in me, my spiritual growth. We have corresponded for a number of years in email regarding theology and philosophy.

Professor Cary responded: It seems to me in your fully sane moments, you're learning to think in a theologically sounder way—for example, you're less prone to read Scripture as if God is out to get you. But you still have moments when your anger, fear or paranoia take over. From where I sit, these moments seem less likely to be part of how you actually think than before. It seems that sometimes you just give in to the residual paranoia. When that happens, I just let it blow over until you can get back to the healthy version of yourself. That's where you're learning something, and (so far as I can tell) strengthening something healthy and thoughtful.[6] [End of Phil Cary on my spiritual condition]

5. Phil Cary, email to author, 2/08/2022.
6. Phil Cary, email to author, 4/20/2022.

My relationship with the church influences my daily spiritual condition. I believe in the divinity of Christ and appreciate pastoral teachings on the Christian belief of the Holy Trinity. For descriptions of the full divinity of Christ, his holy divine nature from before the foundation of the world, (John 17:24 ESV), I recommend the book, *The Nicene Creed: An Introduction*, by Phillip Cary.[7] I also believe in God's kingdom, the heavenly kingdom. (Luke 11:2 ESV). We are not all equal. Jesus Christ is Lord; God is King.

My spiritual condition has benefited when I acquired a personal consciousness of responsibility for my own ethics, morals, and values—this has changed my life's direction. As I mentioned in a previous chapter, recognizing my own sin was beneficial, when I could then seek forgiveness from God. Unrepentant sin is a heavy weight upon one's shoulders. Being told that I am forgiven released me from such a heavy burden. Along with this is becoming conscious of responsibility in my work, how I could assist other human beings, specifically, others who suffer from mental illness and this gave me a sense of purpose. This is why I write. Writing is a gift from God, a talent from God, and is to be used for God's purposes.

Along with learning and the transformation resulting from that, there is spiritual healing in other forms. There are many ways to find spiritual healing. I found that one is to listen to good music, various kinds of songs which uplift and heals the soul. In addition, watching classical ballet videos on YouTube is also spiritually uplifting—the beauty, grace, and energy of disciplined female ballerinas and male ballet dancers, who've dedicated a portion of their lives for aesthetic creation. Just *seeing* the self-disciplined dancers helps me by their precise freedom of movement. I become more self-disciplined, myself, by seeing their examples and watching the dancers as role models. We all need good examples in front of us every day to emulate. I particularly love the Boston Ballet's performance of George Balanchine's stunning *Serenade*. Their artistry is very moving for me, spiritually, and emotionally. It brings healing. The same is true for many other videos of ballet dance.

7. Cary, *Nicene Creed*.

In order to understand the nature of spiritual healing we must first have the right understanding of the nature and source of the disease. From the beginning of my life, the conflict involved evil forces, beings, or spirits, that had a goal to destroy me or hinder my development. It goes to show that the solution is to find some protection and defense. I found such things in my religious faith which included association with Christian people, as well as aesthetic beauty I could appreciate and meditate on.

Conclusion

MY WRITING ABILITY IS a gift from God. I hope I am using it for God's good purposes and that it points to God, bringing glory to him, alone.

God knows how to bring good out of evil. Some people have tried to afflict me, to harm me; but God brought good out of tragedy. Indeed, the transformation even brought about a greater good than if the evil had never been. And a personal strength arose out of the battles against forces which tried to harm me. God, in his mercy, revealed his strength of good over evil as he intervened in my daily life events.

In this booklet, I have explained how devastated my life became due to a disturbing early home environment, cult involvement, and subsequent mental illness which also brought on poverty. I explained how several factors which influenced one another almost prevented me from living a meaningful life. With God's help I persevered, and was able to overcome some major obstacles. Yet, even now there is a cross to carry. I have a lot of physical pain which, sometimes, makes me feel like calling it quits. I remind myself that enduring this pain is another way I need to carry my cross. I need to rise above this affliction and carry on. My church ministry work which I founded, *Mental Health Initiatives (MHI)*, helps me to refocus and live for God and those who need a helping hand. Writing is amazingly therapeutic; there is much less pain when I am at the keyboard, typing.

Through belief in God and my spiritual practices I was able to gain better mental health. The church, with many of Christ's body in the field of medicine in the form of physicians and therapists, were an influence to promote healing which took place over a course of many years. Not only a healing of my psychological health; but healing in relationships and physical living circumstances. This booklet was to show the progression from complete mental and physical breakdown to the level of recovery to where I could write about the events of the past and show how I was able to overcome certain conditions to obtain a better quality of life.

But it wasn't all smooth sailing. I've been laughed at, even by those in the church. Being of low-income, my financial offerings at church have been for the most part, meager. One of the church treasurers who took care of the offering basket every Sunday used to laugh at me in my face, every time I entered the same room that he was in. I've also overheard gossip about me by church members when they were unaware that I was nearby. Some people would donate something small to help me and think that took care of the whole problem; when in reality, the problem was chronic and on-going, and I would end up in the next month just a desperate as before. What some people give is a small Band-Aid; when instead, I needed major help over the long term.

It takes education. I believe that as people are more aware of the problems that exist for the mentally ill, more will volunteer their aid. But I have found that societal prejudice against the mentally ill is widespread in our culture as it is around the entire world. Here, in the state of Iowa, lawmakers slashed budgets so that the health care providers have little resources to work with to help the ill. And without adequate treatment, many of the patients end up out on the streets, without medication, homeless and hungry.

The media continues to paint a false picture of who the homeless mentally ill are. Too often, I have heard malicious news reporters tell out-right lies in order to criticize the poor and put them down. The arrogance of those who look down on others who have housing challenges and food insecurity is daunting. Someday, perhaps, they or members of their families, will lose a job and/or home due to illness, accident, or some other misfortune, leaving them without resources. Perhaps, someday, the shoe will be on the other foot and then they will no longer laugh, mock, or shun those who are struggling. But why, I want to ask, is it necessary for disaster to strike, personally, before a person is able to empathize? Why are some people so callous and hard-hearted? I don't know the answer. Thank goodness that the religious communities teach to give assistance to others without judging. Thank goodness for those who care, including the doctors, nurses, and therapists. Thank goodness for the homeless shelters and food banks. God's people from diverse backgrounds care, even when others do not.

My psychiatrist wrote in my medical record that my family's neglect of me was "severe." Over my lifetime, my relatives occasionally a little support, but at other times, nothing at all. I got the bare bones. My housing was supported and because of my mother's occupational connections I got an excellent psychiatrist who was also a university professor and writer.

Even though medications for schizophrenia are not perfect, i.e., bad side effects, they are still an important part of recovery. But, medications, alone, will not stabilize. What I needed was a lot of talk therapy, such as psychotherapy; and also, my faith in God. When I first emerged out of the cult, I had a difficult time trying to believe in the God of the Bible. My mind was crippled. As time went on, seeing the psychiatrist on a regular basis was helpful. Although the earlier generation of antipsychotics were not very good, it was better than nothing. My life was under a dark cloud for many years as I groped my way for sanity and a way of life that worked. Nothing seemed to turn out well and I went from one activity focus to another. When the new medication, Risperdal (risperidone) came out on the market it seemed to have an immediate positive effect. At first, the dose was too high, but after an adjustment, there was an improvement. At the same time I got started on Risperdal, I also started regular church attendance. My faith went through a renaissance of renewal and awakening. My writing also got a fresh start. My mood was elevated and I found new hope. I wrote about it and things got published.

To clarify: we need faith, medication, and psychotherapy for recovery from mental illness. And, obviously, food, clothing, and shelter. Social integration is important, though it can take many years: good friends, mentors, teachers, encouragers. A willingness on the part of the patient to learn, think, and grow is essential. Insight is important. The patient needs the ability to reflect and see their situation and themselves for what they are and make needed changes. These are the most important factors to bring about transformation and sound mental health.

I hope that some good has come out of all this, the chaos I endured, the struggles, as well as the triumphs. It could be a classic tale of good triumphing over evil. The truth has been told. I had a friend all along the way: Jesus Christ. In the darkest times, he was directing me. Looking back, I believe I could have died long ago; there were dangers and threats to both my spiritual and physical well-being. Somehow, the Lord got me through it all. And I am grateful. To learn more of the details of my personal history of psychiatric illness, recovery process, and related life events, please see Appendix B for a list of resources.

So, yes, it rained; the floodgates of heaven were opened and blessings upon blessings came upon me—as they can for all who turn to God, seeking help. For God would like all to be restored into a loving relationship with him. Psychiatry, as a branch of medicine, partners with the church to steer people in the right direction who have previously lost their rationality and hope. Psychiatry, as God's instrument on earth, needs to, along with the religious communities, shore up those who are struggling to gain a foothold on not only the basic necessities of life, such as food, clothing, and shelter; but also, to teach the way of peace in the choice of morals and ethical behavior in the family systems and surrounding communities. My personal psychological gains have not come about without all factors working together in harmony; and though people are imperfect, strides have been made within the church. I'm grateful for all the brave people in my life who've fought for and defended the mentally ill. Because of them, I was able to gain a foothold.

God thunders wondrously with his voice;
he does great things that we cannot comprehend.
For to the snow he says, 'Fall on the earth,'
likewise to the downpour, his mighty downpour.
(Job 37:5–6 ESV)

Appendix A

Resources for Youth in Crisis

2022

Example from the US Midwest Region

IT IS LIKELY THAT when a young American teenager in the 1960–70s who suffered from abuse in the home left the home, and went out into the city, there was, generally speaking, no one to offer refuge—no organization, no individual, who provided assistance. Fast forward to 2022. What is the state of affairs as I write this, regarding safe havens for our young people needing to escape a home with severe conflicts which are having a harmful effect on the child's/teen's emotional well-being? I learned that the education system at least in the American Midwest is now (2022) providing a safety net or portal for helpful resources. I made contact with some secondary administrators of our local junior and senior high schools and asked the following questions.

Scenario/Question

A young teenager is in a home that has domestic violence and with, potentially, sexual abuse (psychological and/or physical), some of which is directed toward her/himself. The teen's life is threatened.

The teen wants to find emergency assistance. Do you think they would find assistance if they walked into the police station and asked for help? Would the police take the youth to the domestic violence emergency shelter?

Secondary Administrator #1

I think the police would help as they are able. They would most likely reach out to United Action for Youth (UAY) and seek placement at the Youth Emergency Shelter. This is a short-term solution. My understanding is that the domestic violence emergency shelter is only for a parent with child fleeing domestic violence.

Question

What are the best emergency school or social/civic resources available to help young people who are fleeing an abusive home?

Secondary Administrator #1

I think in our demographic area our best resource is, again, United Action for Youth (UAY). We also have Mobile Crisis, who could potentially be of assistance. If this was reported to me, as a school administrator I would connect the student with our Student Family Advocate. We would place a call to Department of Human Services (DHS), and a DHS worker would hopefully be able to come to school that same day and help make an informed decision. This would hopefully mean a removal from the home and placed at the Youth Emergency Shelter, or another family member in a different home.

QUESTION

I am referring specifically to a teen who flees the home and is without money, cellphone, internet, or vehicle.

Secondary Administrator #1

I know there are resources available for cell phones. Students also have school issued Chromebooks, and the school could assist in obtaining a hotspot for internet use.

The following is the response from a second administrator of whom I asked the same questions, including what would happen if the teen walked into a police station and asked for assistance.

Secondary Administrator #2

The police would take this teen to Four Oaks Youth Emergency Shelter. The school cannot get students into that placement but police officers can, which is why when students do reach out to us and tell us they do not feel safe at home we call the police to take them to the shelter. From there the school would make sure this student was connected with services through our Student Family Advocates (SFA) such as McKinney-Vento services, therapy through a school therapist of United Action for Youth (UAY) for family mediation or therapy. UAY has a wait list for transitional housing for students on their own who are in school or working and a case worker checks in on them. In the meantime (and for continuous support) most schools offer some type of food vouchers, clothing support, and food.

Appendix B

For Further Reading

Details of Marcia A. Murphy's Life Experience
with Schizophrenia, Major Depression, and PTSD

Murphy, Marcia A. *Reflections on the Meaning of Mental Integrity: Recovery from Serious Mental Illness.* Eugene, OR: Resource, 2021.

————. *The Collected Writings of Marcia A. Murphy: Christus Magnus Medicus Sanat (Christ, the Great Physician, Heals).* Eugene, OR: Resource, 2020.

————. *To Loose the Bonds of Injustice: The Plight of the Mentally Ill and What the Church Can Do.* Eugene, OR: Resource, 2018. *Allbooks Review International Editor's Choice Award for 2011 Finalist.*

————. *Voices in the Rain: Meaning in Psychosis.* 2010. Reprint, Eugene, OR: Wipf & Stock, 2018.

Author's website: https://hopeforrecovery.com/.

Bibliography

Camus, Albert. *The myth of Sisyphus and Other Essays*. Translated by Justin O'Brien. New York: Vintage,1991. Originally published as *Le mythe de Sisyphe* (Montreal: Librairie Gallimard, 1942).

Cary, Phillip. *The Nicene Creed: An Introduction*. Bellingham, WA: Lexham, 2022.

———. "The Weight of Love: Augustinian Metaphors of Movement in Dante's Souls," in *Augustine and Literature*, ed. J. Doody, R.P. Kennedy and K. Paffenroth. Lanham, MD: Lexington, 2006. 15–36.

Cole, Arnold and Pamela Ovwigho, *Understanding the Bible Engagement Challenge: Scientific Evidence for the Power of 4*. Center for Bible Engagement: December 2009. accessed on June 10, 2022. www.c4BE.org.

Cook, Christopher C.H. *Hearing Voices, Demonic and Divine: Scientific and Theological Perspectives*. New York: Routledge, 2019.

Frankl, Viktor E. *Man's Search for Meaning*. Boston: Beacon, 2006.

Gladwell, Malcolm. *David and Goliath: Underdogs, Misfits, and the Art of Battling Giants*. New York: Little, Brown and Company, 2013.

Keller, Timothy and Kathy Keller. *God's Wisdom for Navigating Life: A Year of Daily Devotionals in the Book of Proverbs*. New York: Viking, 2017.

Meaning of the Name, Meaning of the Name Marcia. para 4. accessed on July 11, 2022. https://www.meaningofthename.com/marcia.

Merriam-Webster, Definition of teachable, para 1. accessed on July 24, 2022. https://www.merriam-webster.com/dictionary/teachable#:~:text= Definition%20of%20teachable,2%20%3A%20favorable%20to%20 teaching.

Murphy, Marcia A. "Christian Apologetics and Postmodernism: A Rebuttal" In *The Collected Writings of Marcia A. Murphy, Christus Magnus Medicus Sanat (Christ, the Great Physician, Heals)*. Eugene, OR: Wipf & Stock, 2020. 51–60.

Pizzagalli, Diego A. "Toward a Better Understanding of the Mechanisms and Pathophysiology of Anhedonia: Are We Ready for Translation?" *American Journal of Psychiatry* 179:7, July 2022. 458–69.

Rogers, Fred. *The World According to Mister Rogers: Important Things to Remember.* New York: Hachette, 2003, 2019.

Schimmel, Solomon. *The Seven Deadly Sins: Jewish, Christian, and Classical Reflections on Human Nature.* New York: Free Press, 1992.

Sisyphus. Wikipedia. para 1. accessed on December 7, 2021. https://en.wikipedia.org/wiki/Sisyphus.

Trinity Stores, *Dorothy Day Feeding the Hungry,* para 1. accessed on July 11, 2022. https://www.trinitystores.com/artwork/dorothy-day-feeding-hungry.

Zhang, Denghao, et al. "Ostracism Increases Automatic Aggression: The Role of Anger and Forgiveness." *Frontiers in Psychology,* 05 December 2019 accessed on July 24, 2022. https://doi.org/10.3389/fpsyg.2019.02659.